D0562637

SOUTH OF HERE

New Issues Poetry & Prose

Editor	Herbert Scott
Copy Editor	Lisa Lishman
Managing Editor	Marianne Swierenga
Assistant to the Editor	Christine Byks
Fiscal Officer	Marilyn Rowe

New Issues Poetry & Prose
The College of Arts and Sciences
Western Michigan University
Kalamazoo, MI 49008

An Inland Seas Poetry Book

 Inland Seas poetry books are supported by a grant from
The Michigan Council for Arts and Cultural Affairs.

Copyright © 2005 by Lydia Melvin. All rights reserved.
Printed in the United States of America.

First Edition, 2005.

ISBN   1-930974-57-4 (paperbound)

Library of Congress Cataloging-in-Publication Data:
Melvin, Lydia
South of Here/Lydia Melvin
Library of Congress Control Number: 2005922615

Art Director	Tricia Hennessy
Designer	Chris Siarkiewicz
Production Manager	Paul Sizer
	The Design Center, Department of Art
	College of Fine Arts
	Western Michigan University
Original lunar photograph	Used with permission from Dr. Pedro Ré,
	Professor at the University of Lisbon/Portugal.
	Copyright © 2005.

SOUTH OF HERE

For Tracy Smith,
Your quiet language
breaks me open.

LYDIA MELVIN

New Issues

WESTERN MICHIGAN UNIVERSITY

This is for those girls who are sincere & silly, extravagant, heart-draining, excessively beautiful, unflinchingly poetic, and daring: Beth Martinelli, Adela Najarro, and Carrie McGath.

Much thanks to William Olsen for his brutal, quirky honesty.

To the Original Wrankled Poets (George, Libby, Robyn, Bay, Jonathan, and Vanessa): thanks for the late nights, the cheap wine, the music discovered in all corners of the house, cranky typewriters, beer bottles, erect nipples, experimental curtains, naked poetry, and language.

Mostly: Love, to Herb (Herbie Luv Bug) Scott. Relentless, funny, genuine, persistent; thanks for cluing me in to myself; thanks for having the most gifted eye and the most tuned-in ear. Much much Love.

I'd like to extend the most sincere thanks to Lisa Lishman for her patience, trained eye, and receptivity to my tantrums, and to Marianne Swierenga for her generosity and years of help.

For my family (my mom, Carrie; my dad, Sonny; my sisters: Cecilia, Sandy, Selah; my brothers: Rodney & Brian): thanks for the gifts of independence, playfulness, the specific torture of six kids in a small house, of pain, loneliness and deprivation; of perseverance, the cosmos, innovation.

For Racquel. Simply.

Contents

Prologue   11

The passionflower was the first state flower   12

Tiger lily   14

Chattanooga Times: July 24, 1963   17

Marty Joe   18

Holiday Hills Circle, etc.   20

The dirthills   21

For J., whom I never bothered for a kiss   22

Inescapable as aura   23

I know I am august   24

Buried   26

As witnessed through venetian blinds   27

They remind me I am hopeless   28

Suit me   30

Notes on Gustav Klimt's Mother and Child   31

The sound of evolution   32

Nothing more   33

Pass with care   35

Half moon   38

70°   39

For Doug, who sometimes believes
    himself to be Uncle Sam   40

South Haven snap shot   41

Once :: Lonely   42

Don's Oak Street Market   43

June   45

The wrong things   46

Because I've finally refused singing   48

Distance   50

Delayed   51

Sign. Signifier. Signify. Signified:
    an American African ghazal   53

Stiff underwater   55

And who's afraid?   56

The reality principle   57

Stand by!: an exquisite corpse   58

South of here   59

An elegy for the lamenters of dying   60

Moons trapped behind   61

Damned to the air   62

From under that yellow half-moon
    late-risen and swollen   65

Sympathy, my friend: a disease,   67

Acknowledgments

Thanks to the following journals for publishing these poems. Some titles have changed, and poems have been revised.

Baltimore Review: "Because I've finally refused singing"

Coal City Review: "Buried," "Notes on Gustav Klimt's *Mother and Child*"

Concrete Wolf: "June"

Crab Orchard Review: "Sign. Signifier. Signified. An American African ghazal"

Cream City Review: "Delayed," "And who's afraid?"

Diner: "Moons trapped behind," "South of here"

Dogwood: A journal of poetry & prose: "Distance"

Full Circle (www.fullcirclejrnl.com): "Stiff underwater," "The reality principle"

Hubbub: "The sound of evolution"

Midwest Quarterly: "Half moon"

mojo risin': "Blazing and delicious," (here as "Prologue"), "In defense of dying" (here as "An elegy for the lamenters of dying"), "For J., whom I never bothered for a kiss"

Obsidian III: "*Chattanooga Times:* July 24, 1963," "Don's Oak Street Market," "They remind me I am hopeless"

The Poetry Miscellany: "Nothing more"

Prairie Schooner: "From under that yellow half-moon late-risen and swollen," "70 degrees in Spring," (here as "70"), "Tiger lily"

Shade: An Anthology: "Suit me," "The dirthills,"

Sundog: The Southeast Review: "Inescapable as aura"

"I know I am august" appeared in the 1999 chapbook *What's on Tap: The World of Female Voice: Poetry & Song, An Artist's Community Project*, edited by Nicole Battenburg with a grant from the Kalamazoo Arts Council.

"Stiff underwater" was reprinted in *The Best of Full Circle: A Journal of Poetry & Prose*.

There is nothing of pity
here. Nothing
of sympathy.

"A Poem for Willie Best"
—LeRoi Jones

Prologue

I certainly don't think
    we'll last much longer
than the misshapen beauty of a nebula,

quasi-star patterns disfigured by hazes
    of fogs, gusts of certain slow
deaths so deep they build

asymmetrical maps: Cleveland, OH
    to Cleveland, TN is only 4 kilometers
by way of mid-stomach to upper

thigh—in reality, the distance
    frightens my town, Chattanooga.
Here, confederate soldiers ghost about

in Jewish cemeteries.

The passionflower was the first state flower

Every time I write about irises in the summertime,
my mother breezes her way into my syntax, a verbal play,

a premeditated semi-colon, a parenthesis of white skirts,
a nurse's uniform; the only color gleaming through her façade

is her hair, pulled back tight as silence, persistent as hints
of coded language: no coloreds allowed, no coloreds allowed, no

coloreds anywhere, color erased from every visible surface, or fine-
tuned
into the metaphor of the week. See my mother there? A quotation
mark

of respectability, no hair out of place, and half a dozen children
with invisible whips marking their backs and ankles for days, red
whips

puckering through the whitest socks, the whitest panties, the odor
of bleach alone should have been enough to send the neighbors to the
police.

Something's afoot, they could have said.
But they were white people stealing the sun from its sky. White people

dying to be just a dozen shades darker. White people devastating the
sun of its rays. And we: devastating the color from our clothes, the
very sweat of whiteness

persistently mouthing: "Niggers here." In a town where the purest
white
iris replaces the passionflower without a fight, in a town where the
memory

of black bodies dangling like neglected daisies from the Walnut Street
    bridge
is covered in blue paint and new wooden planks, in a town where wild

grass hides the shut down black schools, who could own up to such
    resentment,
the shame of wanting to be one shade darker, one shade closer.

Our hair struggling to be free of rubber bands reminded us of our place,
the one strand never anticipating the braid of switches, the sting of a
    thousand swipes,

an arm angrier and heavier than the tiny mother delivering the blows.
The one woman, reeking of bleach, swearing, "Baby, this is gonna hurt me

more than it's gonna hurt you.
I promise. Okay?"

Tiger lily

1.

It was 1939, not quite 1940; Alexander Hill's small kitchen
welcomed my mother's birth. Wild Duck clusters
separated from the Tiffin Galaxy before the sun completed
its full revolution. Maybe the sun foresaw Mr. Hill's foot
before my grandmother, but they felt the impact simultaneously.

Listen to what I'm saying here:
It's thirty-three hours before 1940;

my mother enters the world on an eggshell-white
kitchen floor. Her first kicking only complimented by the first whispers
of *nigger* sloshing through blood, footprints, ammonia
and a two-and-a-half minute old baby. The earth pauses

to take notice, accepts its responsibility to love my mother
two-and-a-half minutes more than the rest of the world.

2.

1960, some small town in Kentucky—Paducah or such—
a scene so simple the final lunar eclipse
of the decade makes an appearance.

A small diner on the route to Chattanooga, Tennessee,
the "no coloreds" sign politely removed the year before.
There's my mother, the only colored in the joint, hair
smelling like sweat and wild sunshine.

The waitress wears white and pink; her name tag overburdened
with butterflies and cat whiskers: Holly,
somewhere in the middle, seems friendly enough;
Holly can't or won't serve my mother,

(we can call my mother "Carrie" now.)

Young Holly refuses Carrie on the other side of the counter.
The fat man in plaid at the end of the counter sizes Carrie up:
It's hotter than the innards of them there piglets
you serving hanh, Holly? The man could be skinny with slicked-
back hair, but it doesn't matter anymore;
he's white, and the "no coloreds allowed" sign removed
the year before still lingers: *Get the hell outta here*
nigger, you hear me gal? We don't want us no trouble.

Carrie can't believe in their spirits, so orders a burger, fries, and a bottle
of Coca-Cola to go; looks deep and direct into the fat man's eyes;
some kid calls her nigger and kicks her in the knees.
Carrie steps slowly outside, tells the bus driver:

Put the bus in park and shut down the engine.
I ain't leaving here without my food.

3.

Holiday Hills Circle and the magnolia blossoms are not in bloom.
Their cupped white hands have fallen brown. It's autumn.

Carrie and her husband have moved their six wild
nigger babies into the all-white neighborhood, affecting
property values. It is 1978; residents begin packing
their bags, remove all their belongings.

She wonders how many more times the cosmos will protect her,
will ignore the rest of the world to wrap around her. Her children, naked,
stand in the night, feel the pulse of stars in their hair,

the breath of grass in their feet. Each child opens her mouth, holds
   out
her tongue, waits for the moon to pause.

4.

Carrie, the day you were born was house-cleaning day
at the Hills'; the wind's hand momentarily paused; leafless trees
shifted. The sun unexpectedly appeared in Chattanooga to witness

your entrance into this world, then bowed to baptize your forehead.
I'd like to believe you received your first stellular kiss
exactly twenty-two seconds before that kick shifted your tiger lily heart.
Can I tell you?

Here under the maple trees of the Midwest, I finally begin.

Chattanooga Times: July 24, 1963

On his sixteenth birthday he caught a bullet
in his left shoulder. Stealing cokes from a corner
grocery; the owner, another white guy,
another diminishing white town—the town
losing itself, resisting possibilities: sunny day
rains, scarlet begonias thrashing in dirt, & boys
stealing hot cokes. The cokes fizz-free, the cokes
for whites only. Coca-Cola calls my father
by name: Sonny; Sonny with the sunshine smile;
the smile even charms clouds. Sonny who can't
remember what the white man looked like, where
the bullet entered, but how it burned him awake.
Invisible boy no longer. Shards of glass swim
furiously, frantically in soda and dust.

Marty Joe

You loved her too much to attend her funeral,
knocked over the first old lady you saw, snatched her faithful
handbag and hijacked a parked Chevy, rusted & locked
down, like you. You phoned from the cop-corner, updated
me on your whereabouts, your voice like dogwood blossoms
falling on a wet sidewalk. You promised you'd be back
in jail soon, back to one call a week, two hours of TV time, three
hours for meal, four for games and exercise, countless hours,
reflection hours, memory hours, longing hours, hours of
desire for more than numbers identifying you, fifteen numbers
obscuring you, forgetting all about time; losing your senses
is a cosmic loss, like the countless black men serving more time
than McDonald's serves up fries. Lost time. Unrecordable
time, seemingly avoidable time. Like the time my own father
had to beg his mother to give him back time, had to promise
to never take his lifetime for granted. But you've got jokes
of numbers on hold, waiting in the wings, like a love
who doesn't close her doors, the love of possibilities—
first kiss, first carjack, first midnight walk, first fuck—
but first things first, you had to mug a woman, steal a car,
get yourself arrested for assault and theft, a third strike,
and then the possibilities, one call a week, one hour, one voice,
one love and the smoke of a past clogged with teenage love,
the assault of nostalgia. It's been nearly twenty years
since our knees first touched; back then I was thirteen
and desperate for an interlude, for the backbreaking
kind of love that halts time; the kind of time I thought my father
owned, that now time, that money time; the kind of time
my mother sang through secrets: Time's too short for lost love, baby.
Don't you see, I was the death flower with an orchid in my ear.
You could have been anyone at risk, but you wrapped a broken bicycle
chain around my ring finger, made cosmic promises of love
on the rocks, stellar reconciliations. We were without history then,
broken and drunk, a redundancy of stolen cars, small time
crimes, petty drugs, and more hickeys than I could hide.

But then you sold me to your uncle, promised me to cellmates
for cigarettes, kidnapped me first in real time then dream time,
no time like the present, baby, but the past, a future of empty
beer cans, raised hands, painful kisses, fractures, racing ourselves.
The foolishness of youth, of downtown Krystals, of numbers burned
too deep in the heart. Every year like clockwork you woke
nightmaring water's lack, sweated through early morning birds,
winter's brewed memories, and years later, I would describe
facial features and hand tics, the aura of despair, phone calls.
I'm no longer the girl you remember, can't save you from your own
    blood
memories, not the girl to protect you from the coffin holding your aunt,
the last woman bound to you by blood, leaving you desperately and
    utterly alone

Holiday Hills Circle, etc.

Silence.
Willow trees sweep the ground, magnolia
leaves drown the lawn, pollen particles fragment
gloom. Outside noise shatters. Listen: reminders
of pain are what I can't talk about. A shoe
left in the driveway after dark. The heavy weather
of June, despair. Once, my mother shut me up
in a drawer and forgot me for days. Later,
she chastised me for crying. And then, for choking
back my own sobs. Once, I believed people
built brick walls to protect their hearts. Later,
I combed the neighborhood for mortar. A heavy
spade. Love doesn't get any better than this.

The dirthills

Chiggers attached to stomachs, crickets hanging
from careless heads. Exposed children,
no pubic hair, and nubs for breasts. The day
I brought the Bible we had just enough.

Mike was Adam. Beth, Eve. Sean played Abel.
Kimmie, Cain. I was the designated God,
the forbidden fruit. My body had matured
faster than my mind, or my body chased

a mind trained to cover nudity like shame.
Like a Bible. We didn't read much Bible.
Whatever happened in the dirthills
would break us. It should have stormed; the wind

should have been fierce. God should have stopped us.
But I was the designated God that day.

For J., whom I never bothered for a kiss

This couch is a bevy of blue jays straining to get out. No branches here. No berries twisting with red juices. I kneel, bury my mouth in the belly of one cushion; notice one jay fly to another; count the stitches. My mother counts the syllables:

you—whip—will—whip—not—whip—look—whip

And his face is next to mine, devoid of color in this junior high school yearbook. My mother wants to know if his eyes are blue. I say, black and white, just like the photo. Another list of syllables spills from her mouth; another rush of blood from my back. This white boy cannot love you, my mother says. His ancestors owned slaves, beat them with whips. The way you now beat me, I dare not ask. He'll never understand the absence of color in flesh, my mother says. So busy with the south in her, she never notices her daughter's flesh ripping beneath the branch. She raises her hand, counts. The blood continues. The jays frantic for the branch in my mother's hand.

Inescapable as aura

The water in the kitchen faucet finally stopped dripping.
Nearly. Always an almost. The consistency

of looking in the mirror as if for the first time;
imperceptible beauty—creases of skin

on the edge of the right eye—almost enough
to make you admit that four or five or

ten years ago you were a wrecked kid, thin and particularly
unattractive, especially to yourself, especially on Tuesday

afternoons when you were forced to out-race
your sister and her friends; your sister's

pace out-runs you, but allows you to win
the one time your father appears at a track meet;

you faint at the finish line, thirsty and first,
dry-throated and salting around the forehead,

nearly looking like your father after a day of working
in the yard, trimming oaks, picking magnolia fruit, picking

himself out of the grass, out of holes in the fence,
almost long enough to make his wife happy, long enough

to not talk that day, trimming and weeding and cutting
and eventually looking over at his wife, stooping

and frowning over a patch of wild dandelions, a patch
of wild onions growing furiously, weary along the sidewalk.

I know I am august

Am I disjointed? Did I pour myself
through a plastic colander?
My life is misguided
by practical unknowns. At times
I live by quotes.
My personal favorite, *Fuck it,*
dates back to a 16th century monk.

Don't believe I enjoy this.
The lush terrain of truths. Example:
I desire women.
I fuck men.
What *is* a zone, an entire universe?
Check this fact: I am
a cosmos. Oh, the superstitious counterfeit.

You want to know what did it
for me? What finally altered me?
It was Prince
changing his name like that!
That's a lie. I think

a thousand changes occur
every other good day, but I can't
remember ever *being*. See,
I'm trying to tell you
everything, nothing. All things
considered, I dream of teeth
chipping my gums, impotent
lonely little dreams.

I once believed my life path
number was 7. That means
:loner, in touch with god,

mysterious. It means I could be
Marilyn Monroe, JFK, Versace
and Princess Di. None of these people
are black. What a relief
to find out I'm 8!
I could've said (with much
grandiose ambition) I feel white
inside. I could also say I feel femi-
masculine. Or I could sit
on my couch of arrogance.

Look, my hair resembles worms
on vacation. All else remains unsaid.

Buried

Sitting in the crook of a tree I saw my first naked woman;
she was an orange leaf in summertime, blundering

around my thirteen-year old breasts, my ten-year old body.
My ass hurt in the notch of the tree. And Luce, moaning

like only a twelve-year old girl moans, shoved her tongue in
my belly button. It was then I knew how to belong

to someone else. I believe I thought of Barbie that day.
I believe I should have thought of Barbie.

I thought of my mother and father. The wedding
and make-believe children. The children & wedding

they'd planned for all their girls. The jewels
my father said were locked deep between

our child thighs in a treasure chest. And the loss
of the thousand dollars he promised his last two

virgin daughters, if only we'd swallow the key.

As witnessed through venetian blinds

Strange breezes, faulty branches, an occasional gift
of ice, weighty. We live in frailty. Not much like pine

needles, named after a familiar sting, a dangerous
bristling. I think of god in tiny objects or large. Functional

but barely functioning. Cushions, for instance,
on this couch are not god, but the crimson and gold-green stripes

could be. Some are violent, and violet. Thousands of cells
suspended over earth, inappropriate and minute. Sometimes

we exist. A girl with a thumb pressed ever so gently
against her nose. A pause. A singular nod.

They remind me I am hopeless

I write on the back of a photo I snapped of myself, study
the face. The shoulders do not belong to me,

but my father. I place the single item in an envelope labeled,

"The Melvin Clan," and hope my parents wonder
when their daughter, the last of six, constructed

such insensitivity. I tell them I am the fifth star

to the right of the Globular Cluster. On earth, hickory
root ash and dogwood blossoms. They remind me

I am hopeless like so much spare change.

Although I've written poems. On the phone, my father says
hearts are not a metaphor for fish ponds. He has read my lines

quite properly, quite rationally. No one mentions my metaphors

trapped in the South. My lips, Midwest.
I almost give up. Did Dalí own a phone?

In the photo, I smile so hard my cheekbones miss the shot

and my head's top half has vanished. My father wants to know what
     remains
of a person when half her head is gone. My eyes are my mother's

and her mother's. I feel a kinship.

White men often suggest I'm South African, insist
my parents must be the black Africans. My father laughs, "Tell them,
     yes,

my daughter, from the belly of tigers, the jungle of treeless leaves; no,

no, the dark vastness!" On the photo, I do not write: Me, before I lost
thirty pounds. I want them to wonder if, in absence, I've gained.

Perhaps they sit together on their porch today, a beautiful idiom

of sweet iced tea and red velvet cake, watching butterflies
chase their new child, a Schnauzer. Perhaps they speak candidly

about their child's displaced cheekbone lounging in someone's drawer.

Suit me

On Thursdays I wear pants other men have worn.
As if pants make the man.
I dally in my walk, no pen or memory to rescue
from loss. Because I've become my mother, I rifle
through evicted furniture. Something waits to stab
the finger. I dig with purpose, gustily.
I, my father's impersonator, walk dangerously close
to undertaking an understanding.
I have misplaced my gender.
I love, for example, Mary Ruefle. Or june.
In men's undies, I can own both loves, no?
Later, there will be a refrain: why are my keys
in your purse? Watch for the emotional crawl.
Watch the female speak.
Sidewalks idle dangerously close
to undertaking an understanding.
Here, tripping along sidewalks is not lyrical.
If I admit my gender
is in the garbage, what have I confessed?
Why can't, for example, a dumpster be home?
They will say, Too off-center, or june.
For the next four blocks humps scratch the road.
Unruly pollen reminds of loss and beginnings.
Burnt leaves, we say, or scorched, as if detached
hands dangle with lit matches. Remove,
quite purposefully, green. Remove the dress.
A man backs his car, wants desperately to ask
for directions. If I stop for him, I lose everything.
Stop and chatter with the cat, as if he understands
meaning is homeless. Or gendered.
I am no inquest!
Later, a refrain: why are my keys in a purse?

Notes on Gustav Klimt's *Mother and Child*

Sometimes I want to hand my mother *The Joys
of Lesbian Sex.*

Sometimes I want to tattoo names of nameless boys
on the outside of my thigh.

My mother will probably die before we mimic
this painting: daughter, mother, grandmother.

This is to say, I will allow my mother to die
before we mimic this painting.

My version has made the grandmother extinct.

I can still see her hands grasping the daughter's shoulder.

Her hair is lying in wait.

I trust my mother to stop loving me.

The sound of evolution

And don't we all wonder,
Tuesday could be truth.
You could pack my rationale
on ice in the desert, sterilize
my thoughts, damn me
for breathing the lines in my face.
Or leave me. Who knows
the difference between de-boning a fish
and gutting the hooks out of your tongue?
The sound of Tchaikovsky's voice
in C-minor or B-flat? A train derailed
in Michigan but tracks remain
the same. Like you. Tread under the dirt
in my fingernails, watch an otter wake
suddenly   pause.
Did you know stars are only particles of dust?
They exist for show and . . .
. . . listen to the chaos
of me. I feel like a mole
on the underside of a stranger's arm,
hidden/misplaced. I wonder if we
could be shaped into a work
of art: a flashlight competing with the sun.

Nothing more

for Pédro

An intellectual is someone who watches his mind . . .
—Albert Camus

And the mind watches itself as I watch you
and the space between you and our dinner table. The haphazard

flower, solitary and content in its vase. You said
the couple across the hall from you has turned

their sidewalk into a breakfast nook. Newspaper,
flowers and coffee, you said. They've turned the patch

of grass on the side of the building into a park
for two. Catch, Frisbee and other games

one would play with a favorite pet. Perpetual
cynic. We can't seem to help ourselves.

It's natural the way we continue to fight romance
as a word. Stuck in this rut of learning

without listening and listening without believing.
The couple at the next table holds on

to the mystery, not much of anything.
My sister, when she sings *Avé Maria,*

breaks in thirds exalting a woman she can't perceive
or believe. I believe rain. The way it appears

in doses, disappears when language becomes too serious.
You believe distance lends itself to molecules

33

fighting for more space. Today's rain vanishes to avoid the couple
who found each other under the green awning of a lingerie shop.

You once said we all sit around waiting for a formula
to manipulate language just as we sit around

and wait until waiting disappears from our language,
as romance and intimacy have pejorated

themselves from our lives. Romance becomes critical;
intimacy and desire become something unnameable—

bark porch barbecues for two, beaches and snapshots, novels
and silence. In Paris, friends get married

for citizenship and no one notices the difference.
I've heard of couples in China who eat, sleep and walk together,

nothing more. In small African towns women are silenced,
circumcised when they opt for orgasm

instead of respectability. In Australia the cracked earth
craves rain more than a woman craves

existence. The odd little couple is at it again:
walking around the bend, across the tracks.

Pass with care

When Joshua finishes his night job at the paper factory,
the moon has refused to set. It is 11 A.M. Recycled
paper, factory fumes, kudzu branches stretching
to the sky. Killing the sun. Joshua takes Allegan to 106th.
Follows his unsteady desire to place the moon in his pocket.

**

The signs on the road alternate: Do Not Pass
with No Passing Lane. In Cooper, cornstalks—burnt
and bruised—are pushed to the side of the road.
Choked sunflowers border the dual father
and son hearses parked in front of the two-story

Victorian. From 2 'til 8 Joshua bleeds dead bodies
with his father, infusing them with his own fear
of death and embalming fluid. In the slow season,
Joshua dreams of killing, dreams of pinching light
from the sky, of embalming his father's body with stars,
and often of how the new moon will crowd his pocket.

**

Joshua has reached up and stolen the moon.
Feels its burn. Throws it across his bed, returns
to his father, who waits with a new body.

**

The moon has burned a hole in Joshua's sheets,
burned right to the springs in his mattress.

**

Eighty-five miles an hour in a fifty-five. Eighty-
five miles an hour in a fifty-five, Joshua chants.
He strokes the tube of blood rushing from its source.
It's simple to believe in resistance, his father's voice
breaks and sloshes in the room. Holds air. Joshua closes.

**

The moon is burning a hole in the carpet.
It rolls and settles in its own burn.

**

Joshua thinks of blood refusing the heart; knows the heart
continues to contract even after death.

**

The spiders surrounding her headstone are trapped
in each other's webs. The stench of death taunts the sun.

**

Joshua remembers his mother's face before death
only slightly. Remembers his father's hand
holding the tube of fluid over her left arm.

**

The beautifully insistent symphony of horns
has shifted the atmosphere. The cosmos
are out of line. The nebulae fight
with the constellations. One star drops
from the tail of the Big Dipper. Soon
others will follow.

**

The moon lies on the dining room
table, having burnt itself through
the carpet. Soon, it will leave the table
with an ache in its center. The moon
fears the tail of the Big Dipper
dashing through the sky.

**
Joshua looks into the death face of a girl
he could have loved. Could have taken
to the Cooper Cemetery, expounded on the history
of bronze headstones. He kisses her face; imagines
them far from death. Tells her of his mother.
How her headstone fights for space.
The needle is plunged in the girl's arm. He looks
his father in the neck, remembers the weighty moon.

**
The moon burns its way through the streets,
through the soft, waiting earth.

Half moon

I'm not dead now. A flutter, a pattern
of chaos on the corner. White dogwood petals
scatter above and around. They exude
familiar odors. In some cultures
white means death. Bread sitting too long
is white, then green. Dead, then dead again.
Dispossessed. I've lived too long in that state.
From the edge of this building a crown
of magnolia petals spill into the green of sky.

70°

Because god exists as a blue dragon
riding the bottom of my skirt;
god simply cannot exist. Because
night is as unflinchingly clean as death;
because death is death, a red sneaker lying
in a driveway; because shadows are impossible to trace
in dark carpets; because flowers are not;
because I still enjoy the taste of fingers
in my mouth; because I draw maps from breasts
to breasts to nothingness; because light
is inescapable, inexhaustible; because gray hairs
plunge from every available pore
when bodies become old: we lose ourselves
with life, recover with death. I want
to elegize here: the simple truth of peeling
an orange in a crowd, its juices splash the neck
of the nearest bystander. I want want, to hold it
between my toes, tie it to rings on my right finger. I want
that woman in blue dress and green eyeshadow
to wink at the streetlight on the corner or the busdriver
driving without his bus. I want something female
and insipid: the heart of a man. I want the cracked
pavement of sidewalks to dust and pebble. I want fountains
to leave loose women running, their skirts pulled
over uncompromising knees. Across the way cigared men
whisper, giggle incoherently at the sight of dogs in heat.

For Doug, who sometimes believes himself to be Uncle Sam

—the corner of Burdick and Kalamazoo

The man beside me
is covered in red stripes
    & blue stars. A large white
top hat and a dingy, fake beard.
    I, too, wait for the wind,
but only dust, a smog-like affection,
    rises above my waist.
I confess. Sam's landscaped
    hands, an architecture
of exposure. We wait on this corner;
    The stench of corners, of benches,
of pebbles graffitied into soles
    of shoes, resting. I am sinned
to myself, married to my shame,
    an incestuous longing, mine.
To court my soul's risings, make
    petty love to my own heartbeat.
Sam fingers himself mindlessly, hands
    in beard, along the pull
in his socks. His pain, like mine,
    moth-ridden, holes too large
to darn. No needles can save us now.
    We wait: without shame,
I wait for the corners to surround me,
    wait for the speeding buses
to slow, offer one direction, then
    another. I am exposed and secret
no shame. I will nothing but Sam's
    hand in the small of my back.
Mother, I try saying. A coward,
    hoping for someone else
to shoulder these long forgotten pains.

South Haven snap shot

He photographed the back of me, the hands,
    and the hair of me. The angels angling
the joints of me. The scarred landscapes of me,
    the cars hydroplaning circles to form the eyes
of me. Rivers, rivulets, restive fingerprints;
    the ladybugs burning paths of buds on me. He
photographed the tongue so often I thought
    he wished to expose me.

When I walked to my car and found my back
pointing away from me, my head watching the sun
    lose its grip with my sky, drown
    in the lake in front of me, I wondered
how many lies the moon revealed;
    how many photos till the end of me.

Once :: Lonely

a day full of waiting—
your rare uncompromising
heart—the first new moon

*

what she has learned today—
the three stages of spring—
rain before sun then rain again—

*

alone—(the moon around her)—
a cloud—(a threat, like rain)
a missed suicide—(the zodiac)

*

what she has learned today—
the twelve stages of reason—
her keys have frozen in their locks—

*

Don's Oak Street Market

Three o'clock falls like ice
hitting the sidewalk. Three o'clock
and perhaps I just missed the sun
squinting through trees. Perhaps
she'll call. I walk block after block
of stop signs and bus stops.
The houses so close they seem to kiss.

One block with its alternative
school for bad kids. The corner grocery
just in sight littered with teenagers
and their boyfriends who can't play
on the playground, can't buy liquor
from the corner grocery. What's the neighborhood
got for them? Lint-filled trees and playgrounds
with signs to keep them off swings.

I start to feel a little righteous.
I can buy liquor from the grocery, and I'd certainly dare
anyone to get me off the playground.
Maybe a teenager will pay me to buy
cigarettes and beer. It's a black neighborhood.
It's three o'clock, and maybe I buy the cigarettes
and beer. The kids are probably undercover.

They'd bust me, haul my ass up the street
to the neighborhood jail. It's the playground
boasting the no adults allowed sign.
Anything goes. The cops aren't even invited.

But it's three o'five. The school bell could ring.
The daycare babies could haul ass to their playground,
surround me; crawl on me to reach
swings and newborn-sized slides.

The babies seem territorial. What if they bite?
The juvie kids from the corner grocery seize
the image, call me "bitch with leather jacket."
How native. I feel baptized. I'm part of them now,

But it's three o'seven, and I'm still wondering
why my girl called me a white person trapped
in a black soul. The wind doesn't blow here.

June

When at last the wait is over—you walking
towards me in that red sundress,
your hair neat just below the ears;

when the owl nebula sheds
its last skin and we've both been affected
by a shift in the cosmos;

when desire howls its last note;
when humming throws its last garter;
when the eyes no longer see simply;

(how disappointingly beautiful you are
in the darkness of theatres)

(how appropriately sad life is).

The wrong things

for Craig

We were at dinner when I sensed you,
    felt myself grow slightly wet
in the palm. The restaurant transformed

you. Kitchen scents: musty and hungering.
    Sweet olive blossoms staining
the nose like sex.

 We ordered a German wine
    with a lusty bouquet.
The dampness of napkins under pressure

of glass. That night
    the three of us went for dinner
then some movie about fear,

I believed
    you wanted
to throw me

across the table. Have your way
    with vased flowers.
Hard and dangerous

with Anna watching over us,
    shoving pictures of Paris
into our absurdly serious faces.

When you pointed to those painted
    red onions swinging
on the wall between eggplants and firm squash,

you blushed, asked what I saw,
    and I noticed them,
the long tails of red onions lashing

on the wall like sperm.
    Outside the wind was harsh/gentle.
You slipped and reached for a star.

Anna laughed through the outrageousness.
    I wanted to take you, smack
around the wind a little, let you have your way.

Because I've finally refused singing

And it was only then I noticed the moon's resistance
to form. Lately, I've come to believe

the moon. Come to believe it will finally show
itself. But I'm losing my nerve.

Sometimes I don't understand the gaze of men.
The way any set of eyes, any nose,

any lips, any forehead looks at me. On the *Antiques
Roadshow*, a woman dares

to wear a shirt of stripes: sections of yellow, of red,
green. She's just discovered

her rugs are worth a fortune, and now she wishes
she dressed less comfortably,

less true. I'm not true anymore, friends.
I've never had the guts

to wear an ugly shirt in public, in private, even.
When was the last time I believed?

Now men want to know what I'm thinking.
Want to, perhaps, focus

my thoughts, center them on revealing photographs,
on edges. Maybe they wait

for me to offer up something. What do I have
to offer? A couple of cats

who live in my home, speak unknown languages?
Friends, communication is not allowed

here. Every night I want to reach into the sky
and fill out the moon's face.

I want the moon to finally expose itself.
Tell me what to believe.

Distance

I say, it is poppy seeds struggling,
the hesitant smell of symphonies—
hickory roots and orange peels,
sudden rain and dogwood blossoms—
a camera lens poised on a hip,
language poised on meaning,
desire without silence. It is the refusal
of an ellipsis, memory's refusal
of a phrase. Friday nights & Tuesday
mornings, tomato gardens & unexpectedness.
Pejorative romances, white dresses,
Chinese lanterns floundering from ceilings,
names whispered in unknown ears.
Truth is language, trapped
like wind inside folded patio umbrellas.

Delayed

Twenty-six year old actor Merlin Santana, known for his role
as heartbreaker Romeo, has been found dead, shot in the head, allegedly
by his fifteen-year old girlfriend. His refusal to announce their love
is the suspected motivation behind the young girl's act.
At twenty-six he exceeded the life expectancy for a black man.

On bus #5, the girls mourn, "He was so fine.
Christ, had it been me, I would've let him fuck me
secretly, forever. He was so so so so fine."

Christ,

I'm not sure which one of you they addressed, but I've addressed
multitudes of you: in church pews, strange alleys, on my knees,
in back seats of cars, I've given myself over to you.
It's your turn, Christ. Offer some measure of lightness, blaring
beacons of self-awareness, worth. I implore you, send a communal
sign, a small wafer of consciousness.

They speak with experience of boys in maroon pick-up trucks,
boys who "burn" girls, as if being burned were nothing
more than over toasted bread, as if they could just scrape
disease off with a knife, as if the newly-burnt didn't suffer
chronic, transmittable naïveté, giving their blessing to any pretty
boy, permitting him to place his reckless penis inside of her
impervious vagina. No precautions.

51

The young girls sympathize. The boy drives a flashy-rimmed truck.
He must have money; he can afford weekly cleanings, an antibiotic
    here, a cotton swab there. They discuss their bootyliciousness; how
    they hold
their goodies until the right ching ching clinks. He can get clean
again. And that pretty boy, Run-Run, also on the burning bush path,
"killing us," the latest victim said. They casually ignore her warning:
"Death is upon us."

How can any language compete with Run-Run who is so fine
the young girls fear his face, prettier than they'd expect from such a black
black boy. They're waiting on Run-Run to clean up his act,
deliver his beautiful body from such an intrusive evil. Still sleep
walking, they dream Eden: a contemporary crib of leather seats,
televisions in refrigerators, king-sized waterbeds. They can get down
with feather pillows, silk pajamas. They dream

embryonically of the bling-bling, easily ignoring the poisonous,
the precious body, snake-bitten, spoiled fruit. Already they're back
to elegizing the destroyed splendor of the beautiful
movie star known they call Romeo. They've moovied themselves,
scripted the Merlin Santana out of his identity, rough draft
love scenes of secret trysts, diamonds and flowers.
Romeo lost out speaking through the cloak of his penis, the shroud
of his wealth. Romeo didn't bother signing songs of roses to Juliet
below balconies. His fifteen-year old girlfriend couldn't say "no"
to the penis. She could only speak through the bullet's weight, the
    rupture.

Who wonders what the penis says, how it says it?
The boys were all so fine, yes, it didn't matter what language tripped
down their lips. God, we discount language.
On campus a boys advises: "It doesn't matter what you say,
just how you say it." And so went the Germans following the
        gesticulating
how of Hitler, the cowboy grin and wave how of Bush, and on and on
in history's devastations.

Lord, Jesus Christ, gracious One, the most beneficent, The Merciful,
    Oh, Holy One,
we will repent. Offer us redemption; we seek salvation, but please
instruct us: language matters. It does. It does. It does.

Sign. Signifier. Signify. Signified: an American African ghazal

I've heard Death is a white man in black
tie, a man captive in a trick of black.

I hear myth, an earthworm
moving an inch at a time, urging black

earth aside. Elms in winter
displace heat, turn black

as damaged snow. In theatres before curtains
release and withdraw from black,

music lingers, intactly absent. Silence.
Exercise patience. How does black

myth survive? I hear a black
man in red face, red stripes slashing

through hair is death. Black
mothers in kitchens seduce flour

into loaves of bread. And men, black
as coal, squeeze the necks of cotton

stalks, anticipate struggle, create black
gospel, black blues, black jazz, hear

music's possibilities. Unrelenting black
whips damage-myth their beaten backs.

In Europe the black plague created black
deaths two hundred years prior

to Shakespeare's Othello, the black
moor, strangled his wife, prior

to the introduction of black
comedy. Before the stock market collapsed in '87,

brokers held Monday until it too could become black.
Waiting around for another invention, mail lost

its innocence to black, then black sex, black satire, black
ice. Too clever for this set-up? Soon,

dawn will erupt, precise, breathtaking, the un
of black. And here we linger in black

images, repeating phrases as if they are truth.
As if the structural design of words hold black

like fear. The myths fall in on themselves.
But how we hunt for the blackest

diamonds, the blackest metaphor. Strangers live,
resilient, under interstate overpasses, black

as exhaust and valleys of ashbuds. Heavy as rain
clouds, infinite as nebulae. On the corner, a black

man contains himself in wilting dust particles, jaded
as tossed napkins, spare change, coffee, crows.

Stiff underwater

There is an apple on the table
    no one's teeth will touch.
There is a frog on the stove
    listening for condensation.
There is a 24-hour diner missing time.
There, a violin being kicked
    along the sidewalk. It's out of tune.
There a full moon in the morning,
    a sun on a swing.
There, a pile of crowns,
    and there, a cantaloupe fractured
        in thirds; a crowd of flies swarm.
There, ants, red and mellow and black and not.
And there, a cigarette, disillusioned, talks
    of underwater thirsts.
Something stinks of blackness, of blossoms,
    of bananas, clothes on the line, stiff in the wind.
There in the café, across the street,
    the whores drink coffee.
The coffee drinks itself.
    Dalí? Alive? Yes, and still dead.
There is order. Yes, here. Right over here,
there is order.

And who's afraid?

I think my boots are watching me
or at least following my movements.
On television, a monkey kisses a dog,
or a dog cleans the face of a monkey
with its tongue. Outside, the world
is much different. Wars on abstractions,
i.e., wars on poverty, on spiritualism,
morality, or this year's trend: the dichotomous
wars: either play nice or play dead. Opt
out. All the rhetoric out there
and the moon just nudges the sleeping.
How we rest with fairy dust lining
our eyelids astonishes. What weighs
the heart down resides there: a highway
of fear, a flock of rallies. And who's afraid
of the fbi's most dangerous criminals
list? Not Capital Letters, I'll tell you
that much. But everyone's always afraid
to be the kid on *America's Funniest Video*,
caught kissing the apple, because girls
are too Eve, or elusive. Either way,
girls are just another trendy abstraction.
And boys are not bananas. Downtown, fifty
Santas and two cops. We must assume
the Santas are neither abstractions nor black.
I mean, whoever's heard of a minority
Clause? I swear, my boot just stifled a stretch
or mimicked the long sigh of yet another war.

The reality principle

Suppose U was standing on the corner
   dressed in all black.
Suppose U was standing
   on the corner dressed in all black
in front of a red store. Suppose
the red of the store signified something un-
   red? Suppose the corner draped itself
   around another corner around another corner
around U. Suppose the corner was unattainable,
   un attach able; U owned the red store;
the red store owned U; red signifies
   everything, but not *every*
thing, but a stove with a gas light,
   a fuse, yes, a lost fuse, a light hanging
endlessly from the wall, a grace dangling.
   Suppose this list was endless. End list?

Look. U stands on the corner waiting
for another U to give the signal. The red store
owner closes shop. U closes a bullet
in the redstore man's skull. Another U hauls it
around her draped corner, screaming.
U grabs another U by the throat, and listen,
another possible murder, but the red of the store
takes over the floors, takes over
U's shoes, and bloody footprints
are inescapable as truth, *n'est pas?*

Stand by!: an exquisite corpse

Back then I didn't have too much:
    2 medium zucchini, keenly diced, blossoms,
pastries and bread.

I was seemingly everywhere
    & devoured that dawn
each person remaining

in eight seconds. Traveling partner,
    name your truth.
This storm'll never stop.

South of here

I'm listening for lungs evaporating under coal
flecks; locusts blossoms darkening; moons opening
their mouths to the lull of men's tracks. I'm listening
for the clutter of white faces blacker than March ashbuds;
for compassion, the imperceptible rust
in the throat; listening for mine shaft rolls; the sun
black with grief, blocked by black clouds;
the inconspicuous refusal of the cosmos. I'm listening

for light, but there is no light here. The miners can't escape
their darkness; almost white when they enter the grottos;
can't escape their bodies, black under the blocked sun.
How long will the light refuse them? Who will wash
the black from the moon; from the mouths of caves?
Who will wash the willows drenched in black?

An elegy for the lamenters of dying

In this city nights aren't nights;
the sun takes the longest time to set.
In my city nights are dark and mellow;
the sun swallows sky. In my city Death
floats, parades her loneliness like a lost
river. A pricey toll, Death. A concubine,
soliciting the light of moon to her bed.

Moons trapped behind

for Angela

She was three quarters moon, the undiscovered corner
of the horsehead nebula, a star blinking
itself away, a night without darkness.
She was waterbeds, diffused housefires,
whiskey on the rocks. Asian lillies, oak trees, nude
photos, heavy footed, heavy willed, just plain heavy.
Blizzards in Tennessee valleys, adamant rain forcing
the flood, the unbent voices traveling between
holes in my screen. She was the moon
finally wrapping around itself, tucking quickly
into a lavender sky. The butterfly nebula
only existing once every seven odd years. She was death
and then death & we buried her quickly on the side
of the cemetery furthest from the setting of the sun.

*

Joyce, believe this, your daughter never liked pink,
never wore pink, never lasted through anything
pink. Or lace. Her choice of coffin was burgundy
with no trim, not the white implied by prom night
gloves, moons trapped behind, barely existing.
Was she dead when she stole cigarettes
from your purse, apples stuck between life
from the neighbor's yard? Was she dead
when she drowned shots of Tennessee rain
under moonlight? Was she dead when we exchanged
blood for blood and spit for salvation?

Damned to the air

for Frank Stanford

You arrived from another desire, weighted
with luggage, death. I imagine you dreamt
you would die, alive, in the remains of a dream.
Legended.

**

I imagine your last meal was airline peanuts,
ice water in whiskey glasses and cold tea.
If the stories are true, you must have sipped
whiskey from a plastic water cup. While sweat
poured across your cheek, did you know
your arrival would obscure you? Would re-affirm you?

**

Yes. You had whiskey in a plastic cup used for water
and demanded hot tea in a cold tea glass. Sweat
poured itself down your face, across your cheekbone
and lodged in your mouth's corner. You thought
it was a tear and wrote "tear" on a sheet of paper,
stuffed that tear in your pocket. You saw a woman

who was death across the aisle. That woman carried
your dreams. You called her Death in your mind,
then said her name, Death, across the aisle. She didn't take
notice. You rose from your seat like a man guided by the moon.

**

I say moon because you dream Death's face is astonished
like the sun. Her sun-like face and your moon-filled body
sent you backwards, into a not-dream; your whiskey slipped
like a ghost into the lap of the child next to you.

That child has never been found, never interviewed, but I know
he must have screamed "cold." You rescinded. Screamed "death"
and "whiskey" and "damn" and "death" again. You removed the sweat-
stained tear of paper from your pocket, wrote D-E-A-T-H over
TEAR. It wouldn't matter in the end, but you knew
you would never remember. Death took notice, of the whiskey
damned to the air. The silence following the spilling of language
Death took notice of.

**

You sat your moods down before you. In your poems,
the boy would have sliced the silence like a knife. But he refused
you your similes, petulant, like a strained cloud. Death looked
out her window. You looked out death. You slept and dreamt
of Death's sun-like face and not-moon body.

**

Frank, forgive me, but in this poem, you dreamt Death
pulled a gun and stuck it in your throat like a knife.
You laughed often. Reminded Death you controlled knives.
Knives singing in the wind, knives aching in water.
Death stuck the gun in the throat that laughed.

Your throat stopped laughing. Moon hung low
in a branch, intense, and refusing to smile. Moon
kept fading its face but not its mouth. You wanted that moon
with sometimes face and sometimes not to speak.   63
Moon, too, refused you.

**

The night's stars composed star charade, invited you
as the night's guest. The face of Death—sun-like—didn't notice
the stars' formations. Moon noticed. Moon's face dipped,
nudged you in the thigh, but that gun was still aching in your throat.

The stars formed an ear. Moon's burn on your thigh was so hot
you thought you'd stepped from your dream. The stars charaded
     death.
Charaded death again and then once twisted death so many times
     Death
cried out "death."

**

Death's hand on your head feels like the holy ghost. You wake:
Death's red lips close to your own. Death's body smells like stars
and leaves. Oh, Frank. I wish I could leave you in your dream.
Keep you on that plane. But reality, Frank. You walked off that plane
Like a dream. Followed Death, murmuring, "Here. Death." And then
     "yes."

From under that yellow half-moon late-risen and swollen

for Angela

And when I dream of Tennessee, I see a young man who believes
in harmonicas and dusty feet, women in scarves, blues dragging heavy
through tongues of men. When I dream of Tennessee, bibles fluster
    desperately

evangelical. They surround me: green and multitudinous. I can't ask
for help. The bibles have replaced faces of the young.
Only once, a red bible haunts.

When I dream, mountains walk into the ocean, fish rise
from the sea, hands baptize my unrelenting forehead.

When I dream, it is your death. You lie on a silver bed
with no mattress, only blue-plated springs. Your eyes move
with mine, the springs move with the effort of death. Silver wraps
    around

and engulfs me, lines the thrust of my face. I can not see.

When I dream, you ride through tunnels with your ass out the window,
flashing any passers-by not willing to see; wet roads built like snakes;
two girls take curves like death; fierce and quiet. I dream of stars thrown

at dogs; we chase each other up trees, rise through dirt like wild onions.
When you dream, girls jump railroad tracks in baseball fields, mercurial.
You dream Gospel choirs, ice storms, bare feet plunging through   · **65**
    unforeseen snow.

When we dream you squeeze me through colanders or grate me
so fine I'm only cells within cells, veins liquid and lost; never quite
    fitting.

The wind doesn't blow anymore when I dream.
When I dream, the pastor presiding over your funeral no longer cites
my name, no longer anticipates my return. When I dream,
I drop into the ocean, fish myself from the sea, wind towards heaven,
towards you, Love, hopeless as kudzu-strangled trees. Friend, when I
dream,
I know you are not death, only Tennessee mountains valleying quietly
around.

Sympathy, my friend: a disease,

one abnormal cell rapidly reproducing.
The catalyst of regeneration, pain,
a blemish on the cheek, an eye
refusing to go straight, a gimp leg, a bevy
of biological names, chemical formulas,
a frozen smile reported to the local authorities.

Sympathy, my friend:
an inability to remove the sheet from the mirror.

When I leave this world, I won't miss a thing.
The cheap formalities, the regret of being
what I'll never know, the cusp of something
indefinite, ash trapped in the lungs. Some cancers
are easy to discover. Impossible to cure.
Some of us are left nameless. And sympathy,
my friend, the bill at the end of a long stay.
A misfired gaze, clogged arteries, the heart,
dammit, the uncontrollable heart.

photo by Racquel Goodison

Lydia Melvin is currently completing her M.A. in African American Studies at the University of Wisconsin–Madison and her Ph.D. in English with an emphasis in Creative Writing at SUNY–Binghamton. Her poems have appeared or are forthcoming in *Cream City Review, Diner, Crab Orchard, Shade,* and *Kestrel,* among others. She is a former Jay C. and Ruth Halls Poetry Fellow at UW–Madison.

New Issues Poetry & Prose

Editor, Herbert Scott

Vito Aiuto, *Self-Portrait as Jerry Quarry*
James Armstrong, *Monument in a Summer Hat*
Claire Bateman, *Clumsy, Leap*
Maria Beig, *Hermine: An Animal Life* (fiction)
Kevin Boyle, *A Home for Wayward Girls*
Michael Burkard, *Pennsylvania Collection Agency*
Christopher Bursk, *Ovid at Fifteen*
Anthony Butts, *Fifth Season, Little Low Heaven*
Kevin Cantwell, *Something Black in the Green Part of Your Eye*
Gladys Cardiff, *A Bare Unpainted Table*
Kevin Clark, *In the Evening of No Warning*
Cynie Cory, *American Girl*
Peter Covino, *Cut Off the Ears of Winter*
Jim Daniels, *Night with Drive-By Shooting Stars*
Darren DeFrain, *The Salt Palace* (fiction)
Joseph Featherstone, *Brace's Cove*
Lisa Fishman, *The Deep Heart's Core Is a Suitcase*
Robert Grunst, *The Smallest Bird in North America*
Paul Guest, *The Resurrection of the Body and the Ruin of the World*
Robert Haight, *Emergences and Spinner Falls*
Mark Halperin, *Time as Distance*
Myronn Hardy, *Approaching the Center*
Brian Henry, *Graft*
Edward Haworth Hoeppner, *Rain Through High Windows*
Cynthia Hogue, *Flux*
Christine Hume, *Alaskaphrenia*
Janet Kauffman, *Rot* (fiction)
Josie Kearns, *New Numbers*
David Keplinger, *The Clearing*
Maurice Kilwein Guevara, *Autobiography of So-and-So: Poems in Prose*
Ruth Ellen Kocher, *When the Moon Knows You're Wandering, One Girl Babylon*
Gerry LaFemina, *Window Facing Winter*

Steve Langan, *Freezing*

Lance Larsen, *Erasable Walls*

David Dodd Lee, *Abrupt Rural, Downsides of Fish Culture*

M.L. Liebler, *The Moon a Box*

Deanne Lundin, *The Ginseng Hunter's Notebook*

Barbara Maloutas, *In a Combination of Practices*

Joy Manesiotis, *They Sing to Her Bones*

Sarah Mangold, *Household Mechanics*

Gail Martin, *The Hourglass Heart*

David Marlatt, *A Hog Slaughtering Woman*

Louise Mathias, *Lark Apprentice*

Gretchen Mattox, *Buddha Box, Goodnight Architecture*

Lydia Melvin, *South of Here*

Paula McLain, *Less of Her; Stumble, Gorgeous*

Sarah Messer, *Bandit Letters*

Malena Mörling, *Ocean Avenue*

Julie Moulds, *The Woman with a Cubed Head*

Gerald Murnane, *The Plains* (fiction)

Marsha de la O, *Black Hope*

C. Mikal Oness, *Water Becomes Bone*

Bradley Paul, *The Obvious*

Elizabeth Powell, *The Republic of Self*

Margaret Rabb, *Granite Dives*

Rebecca Reynolds, *Daughter of the Hangnail, The Bovine Two-Step*

Martha Rhodes, *Perfect Disappearance*

Beth Roberts, *Brief Moral History in Blue*

John Rybicki, *Traveling at High Speeds* (expanded second edition)

Mary Ann Samyn, *Inside the Yellow Dress, Purr*

Ever Saskya, *The Porch is a Journey Different From the House*

Mark Scott, *Tactile Values*

Hugh Seidman, *Somebody Stand Up and Sing*

Martha Serpas, *Côte Blanche*

Diane Seuss-Brakeman, *It Blows You Hollow*

Elaine Sexton, *Sleuth*

Marc Sheehan, *Greatest Hits*

Sarah Jane Smith, *No Thanks—and Other Stories* (fiction)

Heidi Lynn Staples, *Guess Can Gallop*

Phillip Sterling, *Mutual Shores*
Angela Sorby, *Distance Learning*
Matthew Thorburn, *Subject to Change*
Russell Thorburn, *Approximate Desire*
Rodney Torreson, *A Breathable Light*
Robert VanderMolen, *Breath*
Martin Walls, *Small Human Detail in Care of National Trust*
Patricia Jabbeh Wesley, *Before the Palm Could Bloom: Poems of Africa*